Culture, Values and Unintended Consequences: A Workbook

Kathryn Alexander, MA

Resilient Planet Publishing
Spokane, Washington

RESILIENT PLANET PRESS
9116 E Sprague #585 Spokane, WA 99206
http://www.whatsitmeanshiftingtogreen.com

ISBN – 13: 978-0692269664
ISBN – 10: 0692269665

ACKNOWLEDGEMENTS

There are SO many who have contributed to this work! Ludwig von Bertalanffy – my first exposure to systems thinking and Béla H. Bánáthy and Peter Senge who deepened it, and Jane Jacobs who open my eyes to values as systems and to Janine Benyus for clarity and inspiration for the main value of the Sustainable Values Set®. Thank you!

Table of Contents

Culture, Values and Unintended Consequences

Introduction

This small book is designed for you to use to begin to better understand your own values system and those of your organization. Values are an inherent part of us and for some are what defines them as individuals. Each person acts from their cherished values, especially when under pressure, but sometimes that can cause unintended consequences. These consequences can be as small as a surprise reaction or as large as a more devastating catastrophe.

Because there are three value systems, which have varying degrees of utilization, and because these three systems run on automatic, they are *tacit,* which means we are rarely conscious of them and so we never question them. The more common they are, the more comfortable they are, so their use and impact are taken for granted and *assumed* to be correct.

This workbook is designed to help you think in new ways about your values and those of your department and organization, by learning to see these three systems at work. Values are an inherent part of a business culture, and as such they have huge implications for the impact the corporate culture has on strategy and strategy implementation. At the end you will find a series of work pages where you can begin to clarify your thinking about how these value systems impact your workplace.

Definition

All values fall into one or two broad categories: moral values and non-moral values. In this chapter, the terms "moral" and "non-moral" are used without any religious connotations.

Moral values have to do with right and wrong, good and evil. They guide your behavior with the force of obligation. They form the basis for judgments of moral responsibility and guide such ethical behavior as telling the truth, keeping agreements, and not injuring others. Associated with moral values are such character traits as honesty, loyalty, and fairness. Moral statements often contain words such as "must…ought… should… never…always".

Non-moral values have to do with tastes, preferences, and styles. They relate to what is desirable and undesirable, as opposed to what is right and wrong or good and evil. Non-moral values carry no sense of obligation. There is no moral responsibility connected with accepting or rejection a non-moral value.

The traits associated with non-moral values tend to be personality traits like charm, shyness, or cheerfulness, as supposed to character traits like honesty or fairness. The activities that come out of non-moral values are merely preferred, not dictated: going to the ballgame instead of to a movie, reading a book instead of watching television.

Non-moral values are a lot more plentiful than moral values, since they are expressions of your attitudes toward all sorts of objects, concepts, and experiences: cars, paintings, art, knowledge, pleasure, democracy, history, sports, hobbies, etc.

Statements of non-moral value often contain the same words as statements of moral value, but examination shows that the words are not meant in an absolute, normative sense. Because we often confuse moral and non-moral values, we can defend our non-moral values very passionately and even destroy valued relationships because of them. This workbook does not go deeply into this subject, but you can work with us in our *Values Clarification* program if this interests you.

In this workbook we will be talking about **very specific** values that are held in a "moral" sense and the three systems these values form.

Values as Systems

One thing that is unique to the Art of Leadership - Impact approach to values, is our understanding of them as systems. Before we get into how we see them as systems, let's expand on what we mean by "systems" and then we'll look at the implications that has as we apply our values to real life situations.

Systems Theory

All living systems share certain characteristics:
  - All living systems have a purpose

- Living systems are wholes that can be taken apart and consist of parts and processes

- All of the parts consist of interrelated parts/processes

- All of the parts are interdependent

- Each part has an affect on the whole, but not all the time and not independently

- The effects are non-linear

- All living systems are nested

What does all this mean?

Living Systems Have Purpose

We are only taking about living systems and NOT mechanical systems. So these characteristics apply to biological and social systems, i.e. all human systems.

One of the things that make humans so complex is that we have a number of purposes. Most biological systems (ecologies) have simple purposes; stay alive and reproduce. Humans complicate things. We have those purposes, but we also want to succeed (how ever we define that) and we may also want vengeance and have other emotional needs we want met, so they become "purposes".

The key here is that a "purpose" however it is defined *at that moment* will dictate how people behave. The "purpose" describes *why* the behavior took place and forms the *context* for decision-making.

Living Systems Are Wholes

You are the living system you are most familiar with. You, as a person, are a whole. You *can* be taken apart (medicine is getting very good at this), but doing so affects the entire rest of the system (your body). For example, if you break your little toe your whole body begins to compensate. That's a small example of interrelatedness. If you are taken apart, that part (your hand, for instance) has no function. It functions *only* as part of the whole. In organizations this is particularly important because we tend to think that each department is important when, in reality, it's the *interaction* between departments that makes the organization work.

Non-Linearity

Most of us think of cause and effect as sort of a "push-pull" affair. You push here and it moves there. There is a direct "line" between the cause and the effect. In living systems that is not the case. Living systems have a *non-linear* type of cause and effect. My best example is a story.

At the Ritz Carlton hotel they had been making lots of changes and were very proud of their results. So proud that they decided to offer $100 to any guest who order from room service who was unhappy. Suddenly they discovered that they were paying out way too many of these $100 "gifts". People were up set because their food was cold upon arrival.

Now think a moment – what would you do about this situation? Castigate the delivery folks? Hire new ones?

Ritz Carlton asked the delivery folks what was happening. They were told that the delivery folks had to wait for the elevators, and that's why the dinners were cold.

Now think a moment – what would you do about this situation? Set aside one elevator for deliveries? Put in a new elevator? Give the delivery folks hot boxes to protect the food?

So they researched the next step to find out why the delivery folks had to wait. The reason they discovered was that the maids were using the elevators.

Now what's your solution? Hire more maids? Dedicate an elevator? Make them take the stairs?

The next research was to discover why the maids were going up and down. The reason was that there were not enough towels.

So, the food was being delivered cold because there were not enough towels.

This is what is meant by non-linear. There is NO direct line between the presenting problem and the solution. By asking "Why" five times you can get to the root cause. This is also why it is so hard to really solve problems in organizations. The solutions are NOT readily apparent.

The same is true of values issues. Good values can cause bad problems and good values *misapplied* can cause corruption. This is true because values from one system – with its intended purpose undermine the values of any other system because they do not have the same purpose, thus creating corruption.

Feedback Loops
Feedback is crucial for systems. Feedback is the process of getting information into the system to keep it fulfilling its purpose. Without feedback the system would become chaotic and out of control. Feedback allows the system to self-correct.

Feedback comes in two flavors:

+	–
Accelerating Reinforcing	Dampening Balancing

Neither is good or bad, both can be good and both can require drastic change to maintain the direction toward purpose.

Feedback that is accelerating could be information about how your work is received. If your boss yells at you because the format was wrong, if your co-workers tease you for an outburst, or if no one pays attention to your report, then you are in an accelerating/reinforcing loop of feedback that tells you your work is not valued, and by extension you may not feel valued.

On-the-other-hand, if your boss tells you in front of others how good your work was, if co-workers ask to see your work, if your co-workers ask your advice so they can improve their work, then you are in an accelerating/reinforcing loop that tells you your work has value and by extension you may feel you are valued.

If your boss commends you in front of others, and someone points out an area of weakness, then you have just experienced a balancing/dampening loop that counters the accelerating/reinforcing loop in which BOTH may suggest that your work has value OR that value may have just been reduced.

Both accelerating/reinforcing and dampening/balancing loops are important and necessary. It is the interaction that keeps a system (in the above example – you) on its correct course. Feedback is crucial – seek it!

All Systems are Nested
Smaller systems sit inside bigger systems. This is a bit of a "Duh," but what it means is that the bigger systems control the behavior of the smaller systems as the smaller systems react and respond to the larger system.

So you respond to your department. Your department responds to your company which responds to your city. Your city responds to your state which responds to your country. All of them *should* respond to nature, but we have gotten good at deferring and protecting ourselves from those responses – and there in lies a tale!

In organizations each department and each level (frontline, middle manager, and executive, to name a few) are all different systems interacting with other systems. This is one reason why people who get promoted into the system 'above' act differently – they are now inside a different system and new behavior is required.

The Art of Leadership - Impact Approach to Values

Values as Systems

For our purposes we look at three distinct systems. The first is the Protective system. Its purpose is protection. There are about 15 separate values that compose this system. The second system is the Effective system and its purpose is effectiveness. It too is composed of about 15 separate values. The third system is the Sustainable system that functions in much the same way as nature. Then there is an additional system of shared values that all systems endorse.

We look at very specific values. Some of them are not values that would naturally come to your mind. Their use is so automatic that they are invisible. As they are listed and described, look into your own behavior and see if they show up.

Protective Values

The Protective system is very old. It formed when positions in the community were very fixed and often hereditary. These values originally applied to the military, government and religious sectors. Now we all have them.

Be Loyal

Loyalty is often seen an undying and unequivocal support. The underlying belief is that a person should be so trusted that there are no questions allowed about the leaders actions. There is no public dissent allowed and there is no hesitation in following the leaders orders. This is the pivotal value in this value set and all the others are brought forward if this value is favored.

Take Vengeance

When some one is disloyal then they should be made to pay for their transgression. People who do not follow the party line should be punished or penalized in some way for their behavior.

Deceive for the Sake of the Task

Lying and subterfuge and permissible if they will help get the job done. Decoys, deception, and other methods of hiding what is being done

are OK if the end is honorable. Think military,
law enforcement and
that little white lie
that eases an
uncomfortable
situation.

Obedience and Discipline are Expected

People who are very disciplined and obedient are
prized and held up for admiration. Independent
behavior is not tolerated.

Exclusivity is the Norm

It takes effort and perhaps
some kind of initiation to
belong to this group.
Credentials are everything.
Belonging to this group is
seen as an achievement.

Treasure Honor

What ever you do, do not embarrass or
compromise others in the group. Your word is
your bond and you can be counted upon.

Adhere to Tradition
New thought is not appreciated, we like doing things the old way. We value the historic and original as the proper way of doing things.

Show Fortitude
Don't complain and don't take the easy way out. Work hard and suffer in silence. Those who "suffer" the most without complaining are prized.

Be Fatalistic
Bad things happen, it's just how the world works don't be surprised and don't expect anything else.

Be Ostentatious
Showing off your abilities, power and success is part of belonging. Status is achieved through visible means of success.

Exert Prowess

Flaunt your skill and capability and make sure that everyone knows what you can do. Skill matters and must be shown and acknowledged.

Shun Trading

You do not work for money, you work for honor and loyalty. Money is not the main goal. To seek money is to dishonor the work.

Dispense Largesse

You rise in status as you are more generous. Giving of gifts is a sign of your status and power.

Make Rich use of Leisure

Leisure should be devoted to the arts or to charity. You should be productive in some way that is not monetary and that gives you public visibility and status.

Think about how YOU live these values. Do you see them at work? Where else might you see them? Remember the goal is protection and that these values form a system and are interdependent.

Effective Values

This system is newer and focused on exchange. These values were found in the domain of merchants, traders and business. Now, however, they are found in all walks of life.

Shun Force

Coercion and force are not to be used to get people's participation. You do not want to make enemies by using intimidation or violence.

Come to Voluntary Agreement

People need to agree from their own free will. Agreements are negotiated and serve the needs and desires of all parties.

Be Honest

Tell the truth and state how things really are. Don't engender false expectations of hide important facts and circumstances.

Collaborate

Work with others to obtain your goals. Relationships are important are partnerships of various kinds. Working together, each looks out for the other and shares learning and opportunities.

Compete

Do your best to be better than others in your field. Grow yourself by doing each project better than the last one.

Respect Contracts

Create agreements that are strong and serve all parties, then keep those contracts as you keep your word.

Use Initiative & Enterprise

Be creative and think in new ways. Be the first to bring a new product or service to your clients. Create new opportunities and be the first to implement them.

Be Open to Inventiveness & Novelty

Be open minded and pay attention to new possibilities, where ever they may be found. Then make good use of them.

Be Effective

Make sure that what you do achieves the ends you had in mind. Make sure that your actions meet the goals, needs and desires of those you are working with and for.

Promote Comfort & Convenience

Establish yourself as one who can make life easier and more satisfying for others.

Dissent for the Task

Openly state problems or issues you notice so that the result will be to everyone's satisfaction. Don't hide tribulations, troubles or problems.

Invest for Productivity

Make sure you have the resources to increase your capacity, capability and to improve the quality of what you do.

Be Industrious

Work hard and be tireless in the pursuit of your goals.

Be Thrifty
Waste as little as possible and conserve what ever you can.

Be Optimistic
Do not become overcome by experiences or circumstances. Know always that a better, more productive time awaits.

Think about how YOU live these values. Do you see them at work? Where else might you see them? Remember the goal is effectiveness and that these values form a system and are interdependent.

Sustainable Values

The Sustainable Values Set® is broken down into four subsets: Commitment, Continuity, Resilience, Fertility

1. Commitment
Integrity of the Whole
All parts are equally important and valid, interde pendent, and interconnected. Which is more important: letters, words, sentences, paragraphs

or documents? Which is more important: microbes, worms, lizards, guinea pigs, horses, or humans? Communication cannot happen without the former and life cannot happen without the latter. The roles vary, but all are equally important and valuable.

Any action affects the whole, but not at the same time, and in a non-linear fashion. One of the big differences between linear and non-linear cause and effect is time. With linear cause and effect the action and response are immediate. I push you and you fall. With non-linear cause and effect the response/effect happens at a later time and even in a different circumstance. I push you and while you recover you push someone else of my same ethnic background in retaliation for my action two days later. It is not always easy to see the causes of our actions, but not seeing them does not mean they don't exist.

Seeing wholes and understanding patterns are crucial to integrity and ethical action.

All Actions Create the Conditions that Support Life
Life is not just existence, but the joy in living.

Actions and thoughts that deny or undermine the joy of living are not life enhancing. Struggle that builds capacity is necessary for Life.

No Action is neutral it either supports Life or it doesn't. All actions have consequences. Skilled action is Life enhancing. Action that comes from the heart supports Life. Actions infused with gratitude and appreciation are Life enhancing. Your body knows when you have acted in a way that supports Life.

Humans are Intrinsic to the Web of Life
The universe can only see and celebrate itself through humans. We are the only species who can see the entire curve of creation from the past to the present and thus appreciate the increasing complexity of consciousness. We are the only ones capable of seeing wholes and patterns and appreciate the majesty around us. Acting on what only we can see and know is key to our value.

Right Relationship
Relationship is an acknowledgement of the value and contribution of the other. Right relationship is acting in that knowledge to preserve and respect that value.

2. Continuity

Precautionary Principle
Nothing is more important than the future of Life, so all actions are mitigated to ensure both continuation of Life, the health of life, the joy of Life and the relationships that sustain life. Attention is paid to the implications and consequences of all decisions. When there is doubt about the impact on Life or the decision appears damaging, no action is taken. The tension between desire and consequences is used to create a new and life enhancing solution. Future consequences are more important than immediate need.

Interdependency
Nothing exists on its own without the contribution and support of something else. To remove any part of this chain is to put the entire chain at risk. Life thinks in systems and not in things. All things are interconnected and as such

each entity impacts everything else in a non-linear cause and effect manner.

Optimization

The goal is to make the whole healthy and successful – to be the best it can be.
We tend to maximize parts and sacrifice the health of the whole, in doing so. Understanding that all things have a season we can learn to work with the natural cycles of growth, allowing for fallow times. Working within natural rhythms maintains the health of the whole.

3. Resilience

Self-Organization

Self-Organization is the ability for living individuals to move in a way that enhances their comfort and sustainability by processing information they get from their environment. The actions of individuals who do this supports and enhances the ability of others to do the same. Patterns arise and coherence is achieved through the sharing of information. Leadership is not necessary.

Diversity
Diversity expresses the richness of life and is how life replenishes itself and guarantees its evolutionary capacity and sustainability.
For individuals, diversity allows for resilience, increased capacity and capability, exceptional creativity and expanded consciousness.

Reciprocity
Reciprocity is the expression of the mutual respect for the value others bring through the open receipt of their gifts. The acknowledgement of value in the giving and receiving flow cements both culture and community. It is exchange without debt.

Dynamic Stability
This is the ability of living systems to move incrementally in concert with its changing environment in such a way that while the change can be significant the discomfort is minimal or almost non-existent and the new stable state is achieved with integrity for the whole system.

Empowerment

Authentic actions spring from the recognition of significant value in self and others so that it becomes immoral to withhold that value or prevent its expression. It is power with.

4. Fertility/Innovation

Co-Creation

This is an expression of the recognition of the right of all life to self-fulfillment and self-actualization, that right is mutually reinforced.

Ecologies

Ecological thinking is thinking as an expression of the community of interdependence, ensuring abundance, sufficiency and mutual health for all participants.

Quartzsite - Feb 6, 2014, 4:36 PM

Zero Waste

Nothing is created that can't be eaten and everything that can be eaten is. Nothing is withheld from taking its place as nourishment. There is no waste in nature.

Curiosity & Experimentation
Learning is at the heart of what it means to be alive. Emergence is an active part of evolution and evolution is a natural consequence of learning.

These are the values that nature uses to ensure the increase in complexity and consciousness that has been the path of Life on Earth for the past 3.8 billion years.

Real Life Examples and Applications

When I work with companies I ask two questions:
1. What do you experience every day?
2. What would you *like* to experience every day?

The answers to these questions tell me:
- What lives in the culture

- What that individual/department prefers

- What others s/he works for prefer

- The gap between the individual and management

- The gap between the department and the organization

- The preferred direction for change and how well it matches the organizations goals

- The cost and length of time to make a change

- The likely hood that there are potential problems waiting to surface

The next two examples show the over all tendency in the culture as seen by one employee. The first one, in blue, indicates what that employee sees lives in the culture. In other words, what the employee believes s/he must adhere to and what is present in his/her everyday experience.

The second example, in red, shows what that employee prefers.

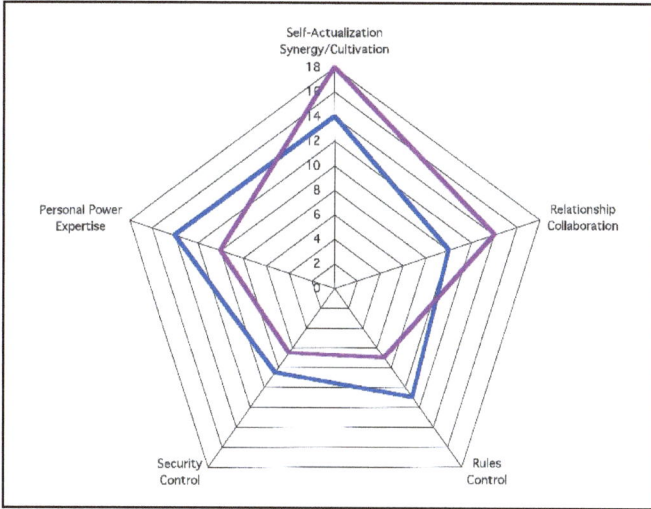

Self-Actualization
Synergy/Cultivation

Personal Power
Expertise

Relationship
Collaboration

Security
Control

Rules
Control

Lived Values

When these two shapes are vastly different from each other that is a good indication of tension and dissatisfaction in the workplace. In this graph it is clear that there is tension between the need to develop relationships and self-expression and the requirement to be obedient and dutiful.

Work Pages

Defining your Values

Protective Values

Which of these values do you see at play in your workplace? Jot down short examples of as many as you can.

_____

_____

_____

_____

_____

_____

_____

_____

_____

_____

_____

_____

_____

_____

_____

_____

_____

How are these values rewarded??

_____

_____

_____

_____

_____

_____

_____

_____

How do you feel about this?

_____

_____

_____

_____

_____

_____

_____

_____

_____

_____

_____

Do these values serve the company? What are
the real results of acting on these values?

_____

_____

_____

_____

_____

_____

_____

_____

What would need to change to make the
organization more effective?

_____

_____

Stories

What are the most often told stories that support these values?

_____

_____

_____

_____

_____

_____

_____

_____

_____

_____

_____

What are these stories trying to accomplish?

_____

_____

_____

_____

_____

_____

_____

_____

_____

_____

Are they useful to the organization? If so in what way? If not why not?

_____

_____

_____

_____

_____

_____

_____

_____

_____

_____

_____

_____

_____

_____

What other stories might be honestly told that would have a different impact?

Effective Values

Which of these values do you see at play in your workplace? Jot down short examples of as many as you can.

_____

_____

_____

How are these values rewarded?

_____

_____

_____

_____

_____

_____

_____

_____

_____

_____

How do you feel about this?

_____

_____

_____

_____

Do these values serve the company? What are the real results of acting on these values?

What would need to change to make the organization more effective?

_____

_____

_____

_____

_____

_____

_____

_____

Stories

What are the most often told stories that support these values?

_____

_____

_____

_____

_____

_____

_____

_____

_____

_____

_____

_____

_____

_____

_____

_____

_____

_____

_____

What are these stories trying to accomplish?

_____

_____

_____

_____

_____

_____

_____

_____

Are they useful to the organization? If so in what way? If not why not?

What other stories might be honestly told that would have a different impact?

_____

_____

_____

_____

_____

_____

_____

_____

_____

_____

_____

_____

_____

_____

Sustainable Values

Which of these values do you see at play in your workplace? Jot down short examples of as many as you can.

How are these values rewarded?

_____

_____

_____

_____

_____

_____

_____

_____

_____

_____

_____

How do you feel about this?

_____

_____

_____

_____

_____

_____

_____

_____

Do these values serve the company? What are the real results of acting on these values?

_____

_____

_____

_____

_____

_____

_____

What would need to change to make the organization more effective?

_____

_____

_____

_____

_____

_____

_____

_____

_____

_____

_____

Stories

What are the most often told stories that support these values?

_____

_____

_____

_____

_____

_____

_____

_____

_____

_____

_____

_____

_____

_____

_____

_____

_____

_____

_____

What are these stories trying to accomplish?

_____

_____

_____

_____

_____

_____

_____

_____

_____

_____

Are they useful to the organization? If so in what way? If not why not?

_____

_____

_____

_____

_____

_____

_____

_____

_____

_____

_____

_____

_____

_____

_____

_____

_____

What other stories might be honestly told that would have a different impact?

_____

_____

_____

_____

_____

_____

_____

_____

_____

_____

_____

_____

_____

Systems Issues

These were: purpose; wholes vs parts and pieces; non-linear; interdependent; nested and feedback loops.

In your estimation, what kind of leadership does each area have that supports a competitive culture?

Department

_____

_____

_____

_____

_____

_____

_____

_____

Company

_____

_____

_____

_____

_____

_____

_____

_____

_____

You Personally

_____

_____

_____

_____

_____

_____

_____

_____

_____

Collaborative

List here those experiences that seem to reflect a Collaborative culture.

_____

_____

_____

_____

_____

_____

_____

_____

_____

_____

_____

_____

_____

_____

_____

_____

_____

_____

_____

In your estimation, what kind of leadership does each area have that supports a collaborative culture?

Department

_____

_____

_____

_____

_____

_____

_____

_____

Company

_____

_____

_____

_____

_____

_____

_____

_____

You Personally

_____

_____

_____

_____

_____

_____

_____

_____

_____

Innovative

List here those experiences that seem to reflect an Innovative culture.

_____

_____

_____

_____

_____

_____

_____

_____

_____

_____

_____

_____

_____

_____

_____

_____

_____

_____

_____

_____

In your estimation, what kind of leadership does each area have that supports an innovative culture?

Department

_____

_____

_____

Company

You Personally

_____

_____

_____

_____

_____

_____

Summary

Over all, what kind of culture does your
organization have?
_____

_____

_____

_____

_____

_____

_____

What kind of leadership does your organization
have?
_____

_____

_____

_____

What kinds of changes would improve your organization?

_____

_____

_____

_____

_____

_____

What actions can *you* take to help bring these changes about?

_____

_____

_____

_____

_____

_____

Personal Notes

Get in Touch

The Art of Leadership - Impact is a consulting and educational company devoted to helping leaders create a lasting legacy that is both ethically robust, effective and financially rewarding.

We provide:
- ❑ Consulting that will enable an organization to become deeply sustainable.
- ❑ *Executive Advancement™* a leadership development program designed for growth for the whole person.
- ❑ Assessments for culture, values, leadership and workplace effectiveness.
- ❑ *Values Clarification* work for individuals and organizations
- ❑ Ethical coaching for both short and long-term issues.

Contact us at:
Kathryn Alexander, MA
9116 E. Sprague Suite 585
Spokane, WA 99206
(303) 818-4147 or (866) 872-8623
ka@artofleadershipimpact.com
www.artofleadershipimpact.com